Principles and Standards for School Mathematics Navigations Series

NAVIGATING
through
PROBLEM SOLVING
and
REASONING
in GRADE 2

Marian Small
Linda Jensen Sheffield
Mary Cavanagh
Linda Dacey
Carol R. Findell
Carole E. Greenes

Carole E. Greenes
Prekindergarten–Grade 2 Editor
Peggy A. House
Navigations Series Editor

NATIONAL COUNCIL OF
TEACHERS OF MATHEMATICS

The National Council of Teachers of Mathematics is a public voice of mathematics education, providing vision, leadership, and professional development to support teachers in ensuring mathematics learning of the highest quality for all students.

Printed in the United States of America

NAVIGATIONS **S**ERIES

TABLE OF CONTENTS

CONTENTS OF CD-ROM

Introduction

Table of Standards and Expectations, Process Standards, Pre-K–12

Applet Activities
    Number Puzzles
    How Many?
    Which Ones?
    Shape Sorter

Blackline Masters and Templates

Blackline Masters

Nets of Polyhedra

Readings from Publications of the National Council of Teachers of Mathematics

Ready to Learn: Developing Young Children's Mathematical Powers
    Carole Greenes
    Mathematics in the Early Years

Connecting Process Problem Solving to Children's Literature
    Annette Ricks Leitze
    Teaching Children Mathematics

Encouraging Young Children to Solve Problems Independently
    Christina L. Myren
    Teaching Children Mathematics

Creating and Developing Promising Young Mathematicians
    Linda Jensen Sheffield
    Teaching Children Mathematics

Children's Ways of Knowing: Lessons from Cognitive Development Research
    Catherine Sophian
    Mathematics in the Early Years

Making Mathematical Arguments in the Primary Grades: The Importance of Explaining and Justifying Ideas
    Joy Whitenack and Erna Yackel
    Teaching Children Mathematics

Mathematics and Mother Goose
    Cindy Young and Wendy Maulding
    Teaching Children Mathematics

About This Book

Navigating through Problem Solving and Reasoning in Grade 2 is the third of seven grade-level books that present investigations designed to develop students' reasoning methods and problem-solving strategies. The introduction to the book provides an overview of reasoning and problem solving as they might appear in prekindergarten through grade 2. The role of the teacher in nurturing the development of students' reasoning and problem-solving talents is presented next. Five investigations follow; each is situated in a different one of the five content strands identified in *Principles and Standards for School Mathematics* (National Council of Teachers of Mathematics [NCTM] 2000): number and operations, algebra, geometry, measurement, and data analysis and probability. For each investigation, the focus is identified, and the activities are summarized. The goals to be achieved, the mathematical connections to the content strands, the prerequisite knowledge, and the materials necessary for conducting the exploration are then specified. All the activities have blackline masters, which are signaled by an icon. These worksheets are identified in the materials list and can be found— along with the solutions for them—in the appendix. They can also be printed from the CD-ROM that accompanies the book. The CD, also signaled by an icon, contains applets for students to manipulate and resources for professional development.

All the investigations have the same format. Each consists of three sections: "Engage," "Explore," and "Extend." The "Engage" section presents tasks that capture students' interest and set the stage for the explorations. "Explore" presents the core investigation. Questions are posed throughout to stimulate students to explore their thinking more deeply about the mathematical ideas. After some questions, possible responses are shown in parentheses. "Extend" suggests modifications of the exploration that make it more challenging or follow-up tasks that promote a deeper analysis of the problem or that require students to create problems rather than just solve them or interpret information.

The discussion section that accompanies each investigation includes comments on reasoning and problem-solving methods and on the mathematical concepts and skills applied in the tasks. This section also offers insights about students' performance and shows alternative ways of representing and communicating the mathematical ideas in the investigation. Margin notes include citations from *Principles and Standards for School Mathematics* (NCTM 2000).

When using any of the investigations, teachers should take note of the appropriateness of students' mathematical vocabulary, the clarity of their explanations, the rationales that they offer for their solution methods or solutions, and the complexity of their creations. Such observations will be helpful in designing adaptations of the investigations for students with special educational needs.

A cautionary note: This book is not intended to be a complete curriculum for developing reasoning methods and problem-solving strategies in grade 2. Rather, it should be used in conjunction with other instructional materials.

Key to Icons

Principles and Standards

CD-ROM

Blackline Master

Three different icons appear in the book, as shown in the key. One alerts readers to material quoted from *Principles and Standards for School Mathematics,* another points them to supplementary materials on the CD-ROM that accompanies the book, and a third signals the blackline masters and indicates their locations in the appendix.

NAVIGATIONS **S**ERIES

G**RADE** 2

P**ROBLEM**
S**OLVING**
and R**EASONING**

Introduction

In three landmark publications—*Agenda for Action* (NCTM 1980), *Curriculum and Evaluation Standards for School Mathematics* (NCTM 1989), and *Principles and Standards for School Mathematics* (NCTM 2000)—the National Council of Teachers of Mathematics has consistently identified learning to solve problems as the major goal of school mathematics. Each of these publications highlights the importance of giving students opportunities to apply the mathematical concepts and skills that they are learning—together with various problem-solving strategies and methods of reasoning—to the solution of challenging problems. The hope is that students will gain a greater appreciation for the power of mathematics and for their abilities to wrestle with important mathematical ideas. Neither the mathematical knowledge nor the reasoning strategies can be developed in isolation. They must be learned and used concurrently. Furthermore, problem-solving strategies and reasoning methods are rarely applied in isolation from each other; they, too, are normally applied together in solving mathematical problems.

Problem-Solving Strategies and Reasoning Methods

Students begin to develop a variety of problem-solving strategies and reasoning methods in prekindergarten through grade 2. These strategies and methods are illustrated here with examples from the investigations in this book.

Identification of mathematical relationships

Determining how numbers, shapes, and mathematical concepts are related is central to understanding mathematics. Early in the learning of mathematics, students identify the characteristics of shapes in order to make comparisons. They look for similarities and differences among objects and numbers, and they sort, categorize, rank, or sequence them on the basis of attributes. Later, students differentiate among problems by noting their structural similarities and dissimilarities. At the most abstract level, students identify mathematical relationships presented symbolically or in tables, graphs, diagrams, models, or text.

Grade 2 students gain experience in identifying mathematical relationships in four investigations in this book. In What's the Sum? students look for relationships between the elements in rows and columns and the sums of the numbers represented in the rows and columns. They use the arithmetical relationships that they discover to decide where to begin to solve the problems. In Match Me, students use their knowledge of the similarities and differences among three-dimensional shapes to identify shapes from partial descriptions. In From Small to Tall, students compare unit strips of different lengths and use the non-standard units to measure. They also explore the relationship between the size of a unit of linear measure and the number of the units needed to determine the length of an object. In Hats Off, students sort objects by size, color, and design.

Inference

Inference is the strategy of deducing unstated information from observed or stated information. Students use inferential reasoning when they formulate conjectures or hypotheses or draw conclusions from their analyses of a problem.

Students practice inferential reasoning in four of the investigations in this book. In Piggy Bank, students use the total value of the coins in a bank and the number of coins in it to deduce the values of the coins. In Match Me, students draw conclusions about the identity of three-dimensional shapes from information about some of their faces and the numbers of faces, vertices, and edges that they have. By measuring an object with strips of different lengths in From Small to Tall and by noting the differences in the number of strips required, students deduce the relationship between the size of a measuring unit and the number of units required to measure an object. (The longer the unit, the fewer the units needed.) In Hats Off, students infer the rules that govern a tree diagram from one or more items of data.

Generalization

Generalization is the strategy of identifying a pattern of information or events and then using the pattern to formulate conclusions about other like situations. Students generalize when they—

- identify and continue shape, number, rhythm, color, and pitch patterns;
- describe these patterns with rules in words or symbols;

- predict from a sample; and
- identify trends from sets of data.

In Match Me, students explore and then generalize attributes of various three-dimensional objects.

Representation

Representation is the process of using symbols, words, illustrations, graphs, and charts to characterize mathematical concepts and ideas. It involves creating, interpreting, and linking various forms of information and data displays, including those that are graphic, textual, symbolic, three-dimensional, sketched, or simulated. The process also involves identifying the most appropriate display for a particular situation, purpose, and audience, and it requires the ability to translate among different representations of the same relationship.

Students can gain experience in both representing and interpreting representations in the investigations Match Me, From Small to Tall, and Hats Off. In Match Me, students match three-dimensional objects to drawings of some of their faces. In From Small to Tall, students draw appropriately sized body parts of people of different heights. Hats Off helps students develop their understanding of representation by using tree diagrams to organize information about objects, including their sizes, colors, and designs.

Guess, check, and revise

This strategy involves using one or more conditions of a problem to identify a candidate for the solution to the problem, checking the candidate against all the problem conditions, and revising the candidate appropriately if it does not meet all the conditions. The revised candidate for the solution is then checked against the problem conditions. The process continues until a solution that matches all the problem conditions is found.

Students make, check, and revise their guesses about solutions in three explorations. In Piggy Bank, students use the number of coins in a bank and the total value of the coins to identify the numbers of pennies, nickels, dimes, or quarters in the bank. They then check and revise the values until they find the combinations of coins that satisfy the problem conditions. In What's the Sum? students might guess the values of the unknowns, check the values with other data in the problem, and if the values are incorrect, revise their guesses until the problem is solved. In Match Me, students might identify shapes that could match given information; they might then eliminate candidates as they consider more information.

Analogy

Analogy is a method of identifying structural similarities and important elements in problems without regard to the particular contexts. Analogy facilitates the solution process because known or easily identified solutions to a simpler problem can be applied to a more complex problem. For instance, if students recognize that two problems are structurally alike and they know how to solve one of the problems, they can apply the same solution method to the other problem. In another example, when students are confronted with a complex mathematical problem, they may construct a simpler problem that preserves the essential features or properties of the more difficult problem. By solving the simpler problem first, the students may discover a solution method that can be applied to the more complex problem.

Students use analogical reasoning in the investigations Piggy Bank, What's the Sum? and Hats Off. In Piggy Bank, students can use both methods and solutions from previous problems to find solutions to new problems in which the monetary value is the same but the number of coins differs or the number of coins is the same but the value differs. Students apply methods they used in solving problems with small grids to solve problems with larger grids in What's the Sum? In Hats Off, students learn to interpret a simple tree diagram, and then they use the skills they developed to interpret a more complex tree diagram.

Verification

Verification is the process of checking, proving, or confirming a conclusion or point of view. Verification occurs when students—

- identify information that is relevant to, and has value for, the solution of a problem (and when they disregard irrelevant information);
- identify fallacies and unwarranted assumptions;
- recognize that solutions are reasonably close to estimates and make sense within the contexts of problems;
- justify the use of particular solution strategies by convincing arguments or—at a later age—proofs;
- formulate counterexamples.

Students also verify their own solutions when they identify gaps, inconsistencies, or contradictions in another person's line of reasoning.

Four of the grade 2 investigations involve verification. In Piggy Bank, students verify that the collections of coins have the given values. In What's the Sum? students justify their solutions by explaining their step-by-step solution methods. Match Me requires students to describe the attributes of different shapes and justify matching shapes to attributes. In From Small to Tall, students estimate the length of an object and then use measuring strips to verify the length.

Developing Mathematical Dispositions

It is hoped that these investigations, which emphasize problem solving and reasoning, and other challenging mathematical activities will develop students' love of mathematics and their dispositions to—

- enjoy solving difficult problems;
- make sense of seemingly nonsensical situations or fix or "salvage"

vague problems by rephrasing them and eliminating ambiguities;

- persist until a solution to a problem is found or until they determine that no solution exists;
- reflect on their solutions and solution methods and make adjustments accordingly;
- recognize that to solve some problems, they must learn more mathematics;
- generate new mathematical questions for a given problem;
- listen to others and analyze and verify their peers' lines of reasoning.

The Role of the Teacher

To strengthen students' mathematical reasoning and problem-solving abilities, teachers must create classroom environments that are mathematically "safe"—that is, ones in which every child feels free to make conjectures, to explore different ways of thinking, and to share his or her ideas with classmates. Teachers must be able to assess students' thinking and adjust mathematical tasks on the basis of assessment data. Most important, teachers must facilitate classroom discourse and ask probing questions in order to deepen students' understanding of the mathematics and of the reasoning methods and problem-solving strategies that the students employ.

Facilitate classroom discourse

Classroom discourse gives students opportunities to communicate their mathematical reasoning. In such discourse, students explore conjectures and clarify their understanding of problem-solving strategies. Informal discussions among pairs or small groups of students can enhance students' commitments to a task and assist less able learners in understanding the nature of a task, the meaning of the terminology, and the appropriate vocabulary to use in a response. Whole-class discussions serve as forums for students to share their findings, make generalizations, and explore alternative approaches. Classroom discourse also gives teachers important insights into their students' thinking.

Students in prekindergarten to grade 2 often share their mathematical thinking in pairs or small groups quite naturally, with little or no intervention by the teacher. Most young children are comfortable talking aloud as they solve problems. It can be challenging, however, to sustain a whole-class discussion among young students. Nonetheless, teachers can foster such discussions in a variety of ways:

- *Extend wait time.* Students need time to ponder important ideas and to formulate their responses. Don't be concerned if your students do not comment immediately. When teachers wait a bit longer than they are accustomed to doing, students often do respond.
- *Allow students to correct one another.* It can be difficult not to respond to every incorrect comment. Constant correction by the teacher,

however, leads students to rely on the teacher as the authority rather than on their own mathematical knowledge, reasoning, and verification methods.

- *Ask more questions.* Instead of always responding to a student's contribution with a direct comment, encourage student-to-student interaction by asking such questions as these: "Did anyone else find this solution?" "Can anyone help with this question?" "What do you think we should do about this?"

- *Support reticent speakers.* Afford students who rarely comment or ask questions opportunities to practice what they intend to share with their group or class so that they may become more confident. Inquire if they would like to speak first so that they don't need to wait anxiously for their turns. You can also bring these students into discussions by asking, "Would anyone else like to add something or give another opinion?"

- *Encourage the use of recording sheets.* For very young children, recording may take the form of making simple drawings of solutions, strategies, or merely something about the problem. As students' abilities to record their thinking develop, drawings become more sophisticated, and recordings may include written explanations and symbolic representations. More-mature students may depict more than one solution strategy. The recording sheets give all students something to share and can help young children recall their investigative work.

- *Summarize ideas.* Recording students' ideas on the chalkboard or on large easel paper helps focus discussions and lets the students know that their ideas are important.

Students' discourse is an invaluable resource. It can lead to a deeper understanding of the mathematics embedded in problems and may launch new investigations. It offers opportunities for students to develop their reasoning abilities as they challenge and defend ideas. Finally, it gives teachers insights into students' thinking that can in turn be valuable in making instructional decisions.

Ask probing questions

The questions that a teacher asks during an investigation can help students understand their own thinking. In responding to these questions, the students make links among problems, strategies, and representations, and they check their logic and make generalizations.

Good problem solvers know what they are doing and why they are doing it. They know when they need help or should change strategies. Teachers' questions help young students develop good metacognitive habits. The following are examples of questions that prompt students' reflection:

- "What did you do first? Why?"
- "Why did you change your mind?"
- "What were you thinking when you recorded this?"
- "Which clue did you think was the most (least) helpful? Why?"

"Good problem solvers monitor their thinking regularly and automatically."
(Van de Walle 2004, p. 54)

- "What made this investigation easy (or difficult) for you?"
- "What do you plan to do next?"
- "What hint would you give to a friend who was stuck?"

Discovering connections among problems, strategies, and representations deepens mathematical thinking and strengthens problem-solving abilities. To help students make such connections, ask questions such as these:

- "Does this problem remind you of another problem that you have already solved?"
- "Is there another way to solve this problem?"
- "Can you create a problem that could also be solved this way?"
- "Can you represent this information in a different way?"

Rich mathematical investigations give students opportunities to develop their reasoning skills further. Students can make predictions, generalize ideas, and recognize logical inconsistencies. Questions such as the following can help students enhance their reasoning abilities:

- "What do you think will happen next? Why?"
- "Do you think this pattern will continue? Why?"
- "Would this still be true if you began with an odd number [*or other counterexample*]?"
- "Can you state a general rule you have discovered?"
- "What will never happen when you do this?"

Finally, through your example, you can strengthen your students' problem-solving and reasoning abilities. Throughout the school day, teachers as well as students have numerous opportunities to exhibit curiosity about how things work and what generalizations can be made, to exemplify good reasoning and the use of varying problem-solving strategies, and to affirm the belief that mathematical thinking is an elegant and exciting problem-solving tool.

GRADE 2

PROBLEM SOLVING *and* REASONING

Investigations

Piggy Bank

Focus

Reasoning about number relationships

Summary

Students find the values of individual coins in piggy banks from clues indicating the number of coins and the total value of the coins in each bank.

Goals

- Identify problem conditions
- Check, guess, and revise possible solutions
- Use deductive reasoning to eliminate conjectures
- Use what is known about one problem to help solve another problem

Mathematical Connections

Number and Operations
- Adding and subtracting one- and two-digit numbers

Prior Knowledge

- Finding the total value of a collection of coins

Materials

- A penny, a nickel, a dime, and a quarter for each student
- Play coins, including nickels, dimes, and quarters (optional)
- An overhead transparency of the blackline master "My Piggy Bank"
- An overhead projector
- A copy of the blackline master "What's in the Bank?" for each student

Apply and adapt a variety of appropriate strategies to solve problems

pp. 32, 33–34

Investigation

Engage

To review the names of the coins and their values, give each student a set of the four common types of U.S. coins: penny, nickel, dime, and quarter. Use the following process to have students identify them: Call on a student to come to the front of the room, and tell the student to put a hand behind his or her back. Place a coin in that hand, and ask the student to identify it. Allow the student to continue guessing until he or she names the coin. Then write the name of the coin on the chalkboard, and have another student tell its value. Record the value next to the name of the coin. Repeat the procedure for each of the coins.

To help solidify students' knowledge of the attributes and the values of the coins, ask questions like these:

- "Which is thicker—a dime or a nickel?"

- "If you traced around a penny and a quarter, which circle would be larger?"
- "Which of these coins is worth the most? The least?"
- "Which coin is worth five cents more than a nickel?"

Collect the coins after you are confident that the students are familiar with them.

Explore

Project an overhead transparency of "My Piggy Bank," or draw the piggy bank and its contents on a large sheet of chart paper. Tell the students that they must figure out the values of the coins that are represented by the answer rules.

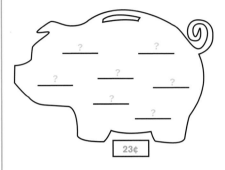

Ask, "What do we know about the coins in the piggy bank?" Be sure that the students understand that the number of coins (7) is equal to the number of answer lines and that the total value of the coins is 23 cents. Then ask questions like these:

- "Could one of the coins be a quarter?" (no)
- "How do you know?" (The total value is less than 25¢.)
- "Could any of these coins be pennies?" (yes) "How many?" (three) "How do you know?" (In order to make 23¢, three pennies must be used for the 3¢.)

Organize the students into pairs to identify the values of the coins in the bank. It might be helpful to make play money available for the students to use during the guess-and-check process. Once the students have identified the correct set of coins (three pennies and four nickels), record the values of these coins on the answer lines (1¢, 1¢, 1¢, 5¢, 5¢, 5¢, 5¢). Be sure that the students understand that the collection must contain these seven coins but that it doesn't matter which coin goes on which answer line.

Next, distribute a copy of "What's in the Bank?" to each student, and have the children work independently to identify the coins. Encourage the students to check their work with their partners after they have finished the tasks.

After all the students have completed the problems, have the class discuss their answers and their strategies for finding the values of the coins. To stimulate the conversation about strategies, ask questions such as the following:

- "If a friend is having trouble figuring out the values of the coins, what could you say to help?" (One possibility would be to check to see if you could use only quarters, only dimes, only nickels, or only pennies.)
- "How did you know that there was at least one penny in bank 4?" (The total ends in a 6, or 5¢ +1¢.)
- "Will one coin always be a penny if the total amount of money ends with a 6?" (No matter what other coins you use, you need at least one penny to make the sixth cent. That would be true even if the total were 46¢ or 36¢.)
- "How are bank 2 and bank 3 alike? How are they different?" (They have the same total value of coins but different numbers of coins.)

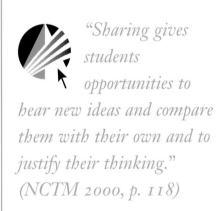

"Sharing gives students opportunities to hear new ideas and compare them with their own and to justify their thinking." (NCTM 2000, p. 118)

- "How can the answer to bank 2 help you solve bank 3?" (You know that you need to change one of the coins from bank 2 for two coins of less value so that the greater total number of coins will have the same value.)
- "Could there be pennies in bank 5? If so, how many?" (Yes, if there were five pennies.)
- "Could there be more than one answer for any of the banks?" (Yes, for banks 2, 5, and 6.)

Have each student choose one bank and write how he or she figured out the values of the coins in that bank. Allow time for the students to share their explanations. An example of a student's work for bank 1 is shown in figure 1.

Fig. 1.

A student's work for bank 1

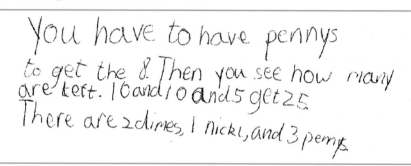

You have to have pennys
to get the 8. Then you see how many
are left. 10 and 10 and 5 get 25
There are 2 dimes, 1 nicke, and 3 pemys

Extend

Have the students create piggy-bank problems for their classmates to solve. Discuss whether any problem could have more than one solution.

Discussion

"Piggy bank" problems offer challenges and invite a variety of solution strategies. Some students may randomly guess and check until they find a solution, whereas others may use deductive reasoning to reduce the number of types of coins, thus eliminating some solution candidates and homing in on the solution.

Discussing solutions offers opportunities for students to compare their thinking strategies and to identify some of the conditions under which multiple solutions are possible. In two of the cases, more than one solution existed when the value was a multiple of 10. The students might explore whether more than one solution is possible in other problems. (Yes. For example, 31¢ can be modeled with seven coins, either one quarter and six pennies or six nickels and one penny.) The students could also explore whether all values that are multiples of 10 lead to more than one solution. (They do not; for instance, 40¢ can be modeled with five coins only by three dimes and two nickels.)

Piggy-bank problems also allow students to practice addition skills in a reasoning and problem-solving context. To determine a solution to a piggy-bank problem, students partition numbers into 1s, 5s, 10s, and 25s in multiple ways, and in deciding what combinations to try, they use their reasoning skills. They can also see how different addition questions are related and how solving a subproblem can help solve a larger problem. The margin shows how students might approach a total of 31¢ made up of seven coins.

To solve a problem in which a piggy bank has 31¢ distributed in seven coins, students might think—

- "If I used a quarter, the other coins would have to be pennies, or the total would be too high." (reasoning)

- "I can't use three dimes, so I'll try two dimes. That gives me 20¢. Then I just need to figure out how to use five coins to make 11¢." (solving a subproblem)

What's the Sum?

Focus

Reasoning about algebraic relationships

Summary

Students are presented with rectangular grids in which rows and columns contain variables and numbers. They use information in the grids to find the values of the variables and the missing sums of the rows or columns.

Goal

• Use deductive reasoning

Mathematical Connections

Algebra
• Replacing variables with their values

Number and Operations
• Solving for missing addends

Prior Knowledge

• Adding and subtracting numbers with sums to 22
• Adding three single-digit numbers

Materials

• An overhead transparency of the blackline master "Addition Grids" or a copy of the grids on the blackline master drawn on chart paper
• An overhead projector (if a transparency is used)
• A copy of the blackline master "What's the Sum?" for each student or pair of students

Investigation

Engage

Project or display a copy of "Addition Grids." Tell the students that the grid at the top is a two-by-two grid, with two rows and two columns, and that shapes that are the same have the same value. So, for example, the two triangles stand for the same number. The numbers to the right and at the bottom of the grid are the sums of the rows and columns, respectively. The students' job is to figure out the sum for the second row.

Ask questions like the following to guide the students' thinking:

• "What do you see in the top row?" (two triangles and the number 6 beside the grid)
• "What do you see in the first column?" (one triangle, one square, and the number 8 below the grid)

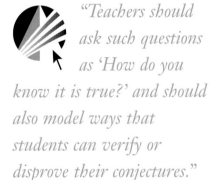

"*Teachers should ask such questions as 'How do you know it is true?' and should also model ways that students can verify or disprove their conjectures.*" (NCTM 2000, p. 126)

pp. 35, 36–37

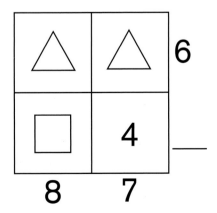

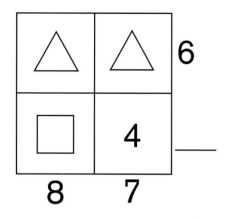

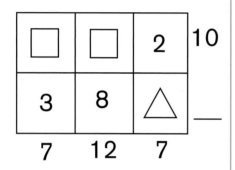

Students who have enjoyed this investigation may like the challenge of Number Puzzles, an applet available on the CD-ROM that accompanies this book.

- "Look at the two columns and the two rows. Which row or column will you use first to help you find the missing sum? Why?" (Many students would start with the top row because it contains only one type of variable; since the triangles have the same value, they both must equal 3. Others might start with the right column because the sum and one of the addends is given; since 7 – 4 = 3, the triangle must represent 3.)
- "What is the value of each triangle?" (3)
- "What will you do next?" (Most students would find the value of the square.)
- "How will you find the value of the square?" (If the triangle is worth 3 and the sum is 8, the square must be worth 5.)
- "How can you find the sum of the second row?" (Find the value by replacing the square with 5; 5 + 4 = 9.)

Explore

Show the class the two-by-three rectangular grid at the bottom of "Addition Grids," and ask the students to find the sum for the second row. Call on students to describe their solution strategies. They might find that $\square$ = 4 by using information from the first column ($\square + 3 = 7$) or the second column ($\square + 8 = 12$). Or they might reason from row 1 that the value of the two $\square$s is 8, so one $\square$ must be equal to 4. The value of $\triangle$—that is, 5—can be found using the information from the third column ($2 + \triangle = 7$). Once the values of these variables have been found, the sum of the addends in the second row can be calculated.

Distribute copies of "What's the Sum?" The students may work individually or in pairs to solve the problems. Remind the students to look at the columns and rows and decide which row or column to solve first. As the students solve the problems, they should record which row or column they used first and explain why they chose that particular one.

Extend

After the students have completed the worksheet, encourage them to make up similar problems for one another to solve. They might begin by filling in numbers in a blank two-by-two array, placing the sums to the right and at the bottom and then erasing some of the numbers and one sum. Note that depending on which numbers they erase, some of their problems might have more than one solution.

Discussion

Problem 1 is similar to the first sample problem. Problem 2 is no more difficult, but it does not involve any doubles. Students could find the value for $\triangle$ first, either by realizing that 8 + 4 = 12 or that 8 + 7 = 15. The value for $\square$ can be found by using the fact that 4 + $\square$ = 14. Discuss why there is only one way to find the value of $\square$, even though there are two ways to find the value of $\triangle$. Help the students see that $\triangle + 7$ (the sum of the first column) must be 3 more than $\triangle + 4$ (the sum of the first row) because both sums involve a $\triangle$ but 7 is 3 more than 4.

Not only do these activities help students practice addition and subtraction facts, particularly for doubles, but they also reinforce the relationship between the two operations. At the same time, the activities help students focus on which aspect of a complex problem to attack first.

Match Me

Focus

Reasoning about geometric relationships

Summary

Students build three-dimensional figures to match various criteria, including some faces of the solids.

Goals

- Make and investigate mathematical conjectures
- Check, guess, and revise possible solutions
- Use deductive reasoning to eliminate possible solutions

Mathematical Connections

Geometry

- Naming and describing the attributes of three-dimensional shapes
- Identifying similarities and differences among three-dimensional shapes

Prior Knowledge

- Identifying and naming square pyramids and rectangular and triangular prisms
- Understanding and using the terms *vertex*, *face*, and *edge*

Materials

- Models of the three-dimensional shapes shown in figure 2. Nets for models of these shapes are available on the CD-ROM.
- One copy of the blackline master "Shape Card 1"
- One copy of the blackline master "Shape Card 2"
- A copy of the blackline master "Match-Me Cards" for each pair of students
- Polydrons or other interlocking materials or plastic shapes that can be taped together to create three-dimensional figures
- Cellophane tape (if necessary for assembling shapes)
- Paper for drawing
- Lead pencils or colored pencils

Investigation

Engage

Display the three-dimensional models specified in the materials list. Show the class a copy of "Shape Card 1." Tell the students that their job is to think which three-dimensional shape might have the square as one of the faces. Encourage the students to think of many possibilities

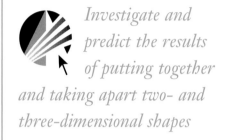

Investigate and predict the results of putting together and taking apart two- and three-dimensional shapes

pp. 38, 39, 40–41

Right square pyramid Oblique square pyramid Cube

Right rectangular prism Oblique rectangular prism Octahedron

Right square prism Oblique square prism Icosahedron

Right hexagonal prism Right hexagonal pyramid Oblique hexagonal pyramid

Right triangular pyramid Oblique triangular pyramid Right triangular prism Oblique triangular prism

Shape Card 1

This square is one of the faces of a 3-D shape.

Shape Card 2

This square is one of the faces of the 3-D shape.
The 3-D shape has five vertices.

and to name and describe the shapes, as illustrated in the following example:

Student: "I think it could be a cube."

Teacher: "Suppose that someone had never heard of a cube. How would you describe it?"

Student: "It has six square faces, and they're all the same."

Point out the appropriate models as the students describe them. Other possible shapes are a square prism and a square pyramid.

Show "Shape Card 2." Explain that the students must name a three-dimensional shape that has a square face and exactly five vertices, or corners. Ask the students why a cube would not satisfy the conditions. (A cube has eight vertices, and this shape must have only five.) To guide the students' thinking, ask questions like these:

- "How many vertices of the shape are part of the square?" (four)
- "How many more vertices can there be?" (only one more)

- "How do you know the shape has to be a pyramid?" (Because the fifth vertex must be at the top, and a square pyramid has a square base with four vertices and one more vertex at the top.)

Explore

Organize the students into pairs, and distribute a copy of the blackline master "Match-Me Cards" to each pair. Explain that for each card, the students must think of as many three-dimensional shapes as they can that fit the description on the card. In order to match the description, each shape on the card must constitute at least one face of the 3-D shape, and the 3-D shape must meet all the other conditions (if any) mentioned on the card. After the students have identified as many shapes as possible that match each card, they can build the three-dimensional shapes with interlocking materials or with tape and two-dimensional shapes.

Observe the students as they work. If they decide that only one three-dimensional shape fits the conditions on a card, ask them to justify their conclusions. As the students work on the activity, ask questions like the following to stimulate their thinking:

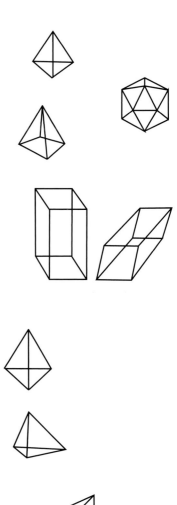

For Card 1

- "Why would a pyramid be a good guess?" (All pyramids have some triangular faces.)
- "Does the shape have to be a pyramid?" (no)
- "Could there be four triangular faces?" (Yes, if the shape is a triangular pyramid [tetrahedron] or a square pyramid.)

For Card 2

- "Why does one side of the rectangle have the same length as the sides of the squares?" (So those sides can match to create an edge.)
- "How do you know that the shape cannot be a pyramid?" (Only one face of a pyramid does not have to be a triangle, and this shape has more than one face that is not a triangle.)
- "How many faces does the three-dimensional shape that you built have?" (six) "How many are square?" (two)

For Card 3

- "How many vertices does the triangle have?" (three)
- "How many more vertices does the three-dimensional shape have than the triangle has?" (one)
- "Imagine that the triangle shown is flat on a table and that the fourth vertex is above the triangle. What three-dimensional shape can you imagine?" (a triangular pyramid)

For Card 4

- "How do you know that the three-dimensional shape is not a pyramid?" (It has two faces that are not triangles.)
- "How many faces does the three-dimensional shape have besides the three faces shown on the card?" (two)
- "Imagine that one of the other faces is congruent to the triangle shown on the card. What would the shape be?" (a right triangular prism)

For Card 5

- "Could the shape be a pyramid?" (no) "Explain your reasoning." (A pyramid would have only one hexagon, which would be the base. The other faces of a pyramid would have to be triangles. This card shows two hexagons.)
- "How many other faces might the three-dimensional shape have?" (Six rectangles would form edges with the hexagonal bases to create a prism.)

For Card 6

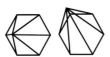

- "How is this card like card 3?" (For both cards, one shape and one other fact are given.)
- "How do you know that the three-dimensional shape has only six edges that are not sides of the hexagon shown on the card?" (The hexagon shown has six sides that must connect to other shapes to make the edges of the three-dimensional shape. That shape has twelve edges all together. Since 12 − 6 = 6, only six edges of the three-dimensional shape are not part of the hexagon on the card.)
- "How does your reasoning help you figure out what the three-dimensional shape is?" (It has to be a pyramid, since the six extra edges all need to meet. Otherwise, there would be more than twelve edges.)

Extend

The activity can be extended by having the students make cards for one another to solve.

Discussion

Match Me encourages students to use logical reasoning to determine solid shapes that can or cannot satisfy certain given conditions. Students are likely to make conjectures, consider the conjectures in light of the conditions of the problem, and then either accept or reject the conjectures. This exercise helps students build their abilities to reason spatially.

At the same time, attention to the faces, vertices, and edges of three-dimensional shapes affords students an opportunity to generalize some of the attributes of prisms and pyramids, including the following:

- Right prisms always have two congruent bases with connecting rectangles.
- Pyramids have a base plus triangular faces, so at most one face (the base) can be another shape. (When the base is a triangle, all the faces of the pyramid are triangles.)
- If all that is known about a three-dimensional shape is one face, the shape could be one of several types of solids.
- Two pieces of information about a shape are sometimes sufficient to identify the shape.

From Small to Tall

Focus

Reasoning about measurement relationships

Summary

Students reason proportionally as they select different units of measure to construct life-sized representations of a baby, a ten-year-old, and a basketball player. They informally explore the relationship between the size of a unit of linear measure and the number of those units needed to determine the length of an object.

Goals

- Identify relationships
- Develop and test conjectures

Mathematical Connections

Measurement
- Measuring lengths

Algebra
- Reasoning proportionally

Prior Knowledge

- Using a nonstandard unit to measure length

Materials

- Sets of measuring strips copied onto heavy stock from the blackline master "Unit Lengths" and laminated if possible. You will need one set for each pair of students and one set for demonstration.
- A thirty-inch baseball bat (or other thirty-inch object)
- An object about eighteen inches long or high (e.g., a large tote bag)
- Scissors and pencils for each group of four students
- Tape or glue for each group of students
- A piece of chart paper or a large piece of newsprint for each student
- One copy of the blackline master "Body Building" for each group of four students
- Masking tape

Investigation

Engage
Organize the students into pairs, and distribute a set of measuring strips to each pair. Have the students familiarize themselves with the strips. Call on students to identify by letter the strips that are the longest and the shortest.

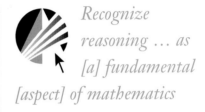
Recognize reasoning ... as [a] fundamental [aspect] of mathematics

Make and investigate mathematical conjectures

Use various types of reasoning

pp. 42, 43

"If it takes eight D strips, I think it will take twelve C strips. No, I think it will take ten."

Demonstrate how to measure an object with strip E. For example, select an eighteen-inch-long object, and move strip E end to end along it to show that its length is equal to three repetitions of strip E.

In the same manner, measure the same object with strip B. Call on students to tell why it took more repetitions of strip B than of strip E to measure the object (the shorter the strip, the more repetitions of it that are needed to measure the same length). Call on students to predict the number of strips C that will be needed to measure the object. Then ask a student to measure the object with strip C to check the predictions.

Show the students the thirty-inch baseball bat or another thirty-inch object, and tell them that it is six strips long when it is measured with a particular strip. Call on students to guess which strip—B or D—you used and give reasons for their choices. (Six repetitions of strip D would be needed to measure a thirty-inch bat.) Ask the students to describe a bat whose length might measure six A strips. (The students might describe a toy bat for a baby.) Explain that the number of strips used, as well as the length of a strip, is important to know in order to estimate the size of an object.

Ask questions like the following about other measurements:

- "Suppose that a table is six strips wide. Which strip—C or E—do you think was used to measure the table? Can you be sure?" (A kitchen table might measure six E strips, but a coffee table might measure six C strips; we can't be sure, since we don't know the size of the table.)

- "A coffee mug is five strips tall. Which strip—A or C—do you think was used to measure the mug? How did you decide?" (Strip A is more likely to have been used, since a mug isn't very tall and quite a few strips were used.)

- "One T-shirt is eight strips long, and another T-shirt is ten strips long. Can you tell which shirt is the longer shirt?" (No, because you don't know if the same strip was used to measure both shirts. For example, a measure of ten A strips is much shorter than a measure of eight E strips.)

- "Suppose that the longer shirt measured eight D strips. About how many C strips would the same shirt measure?" (about ten)

- "How did you make this estimate?" (Strip C is a little shorter than strip D, so the shirt should measure more repetitions of strip C, but strip C is not a lot shorter, so it shouldn't take many more repetitions.)

Explore

Engage the students in a discussion of the relative sizes of different people—in particular, a male professional basketball player, a ten-year-old girl, and a baby. Talk about how the lengths of their arms, legs, hands, and so on—not just their heights—might vary.

Divide the students into groups of four. Tell each group that it will be creating a life-sized copy of a baby, a ten-year-old girl, or a male basketball player. Distribute scissors, pencils, tape or glue, two sets of measuring strips, four pieces of chart paper or newsprint, and a copy of "Body Building" to each group. Assign different figures to the different groups, and ask each group to circle its assigned figure. Have each group select a member to cut the activity page "Body Building" into five sections along the cut lines: the top part of the page, indicating the figure that they will create, and the bottom four sections, describing possible lengths for the arms (from shoulder to fingertips), legs, torso, and head (top of head to base of neck).

Distribute the bottom four sections of "Body Building" to different students in the group, being sure that the students know only the contents of their own sections. Keeping in mind the figure that the group has been assigned to create, each member then chooses what he or she believes is the appropriate length for the selected body part from the list of possibilities. The students in a group should not discuss their choices with the other members of the group.

Each student then uses the strip he or she has selected to measure the required body part (or parts, in the case of arms and legs), draws the body part to the correct measure on chart paper, and cuts it out. The students tape or glue the body together and then tape it to a wall with masking tape. At least one member of each group should be called on to explain why he or she chose the selected length for his or her body part

"I think that if I used fifteen As for the arms, they would not be long enough. Three Bs would make the arms too short, and nine Cs would be too long, so I'll use four Ds."

and whether, looking at the finished product, he or she is satisfied with the selection.

Extend

You may choose to end the activity by allowing the students to "dress" their figures, or you may repeat the activity. If you repeat the activity, the goal could be to create a "crazy" character whose body parts do not go together well; for instance, a character might have a basketball player's legs and a baby's arms.

Discussion

Observe how students make their decisions about the lengths of the various body parts. The students may look only at the numbers and assume that a smaller number of strips indicates a smaller size. Others will consider both the number of strips and the lengths of the units; for example, in choosing the measure for the baby's legs, a student may reason, "The A strips are very small, so even nine of them are not that long. I'll try nine A strips for the baby's legs." Other students may compare the given lengths with their own legs to try to reason about the length of a baby's legs or a tall person's legs.

Students can continue their investigation of the relationship between the size of a unit and the numeric measure with the applet Which One? This interactive activity is available on the CD-ROM.

Hats Off

Focus

Reasoning about data relationships

Summary

Using tree diagrams, students find all the possible combinations of the attributes of objects.

Goals

- Organize and display data in tree diagrams
- Use deductive reasoning to eliminate possible solutions
- Make generalizations

Mathematical Connections

Data Analysis
- Sorting and classifying objects according to their attributes and organizing data about the objects

Prior Knowledge

- Identifying likenesses and differences
- Identifying attributes of objects

Materials

- Crayons or colored pencils
- A large piece of butcher paper
- One copy of the blackline master "Hats Off" for each student
- One copy of the blackline master "Attribute Trees" for each student
- A master set of full-sized hats from the blackline master "Hats Off" and a second set of smaller hats copied at a 50 percent reduction. For each size, color the hats as follows: one solid black, one solid orange, one solid gray, one with black polka dots, one with orange polka dots, and one with gray polka dots. Mount the hats on poster board, cut them out, and attach small magnetic strips or tape to their backs.
- A large magnetic board or a chalkboard
- Forty-two labels made from poster board or heavy stock, six each for the following terms: *Orange, Gray, Black, Solid, Polka-Dotted, Large, Small.* Attach small magnetic strips or tape to the backs of the labels.
- (Optional) A copy of the book *Caps for Sale: A Tale of a Peddler, Some Monkeys, and Their Monkey Business,* by Esphyr Slobodkina (1987) (optional)

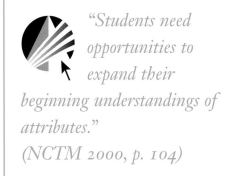

"Students need opportunities to expand their beginning understandings of attributes." (NCTM 2000, p. 104)

pp. 44, 45

Investigation

Engage

If the picture book *Caps for Sale* is available, read it aloud, and talk about all the different hats in the book. If the book is not available, have each student bring in a favorite hat. Talk about how the hats differ. The students might mention a variety of attributes, including color, shape, size, type of material, pattern, and decorations, such as feathers. Tell the students that they will be designing many different hats and that you want them first to design caps that are the same size and shape but different colors: some hats have to be orange, and some have to be gray. Some should be solidly gray or solidly orange, and others should have polka dots that are gray or orange on a white background, as shown in figure 3. Ask, "If I had only one of each kind of hat, how many different hats would I have? What would they look like?" Confirm that you would have four different hats: one solid orange, one with orange polka dots, one solid gray, and one with gray polka dots.

Fig. **3.**

Solid and polka-dotted hats in orange and gray

Next, tell the children that in addition to coloring their hats orange and gray, they can color them black. Remind the students that for any color choice, the hats can be either solid or polka-dotted. Give each student crayons or colored pencils and a copy of "Hats Off," and have them color the hats according to the different possibilities. If the students have difficulty designing six different hats, encourage them to compare their hats with those of their friends. Talk about how the hats are alike and different.

Explore

Draw a tree diagram like the one in figure 4 on a large piece of butcher paper. Display the tree on a chalkboard or a magnetic board, and attach the labels that you have made, as shown in figure 4. Show the students the six large hats that you have prepared. Tell the students that monkeys will be climbing the tree and that they are very smart; they can read the words on this special tree. Explain that they will start at the bottom and decide which branches to climb on the basis of the attributes of the hats that they are considering wearing. For example, if a monkey is thinking about an orange hat, it will choose the thick

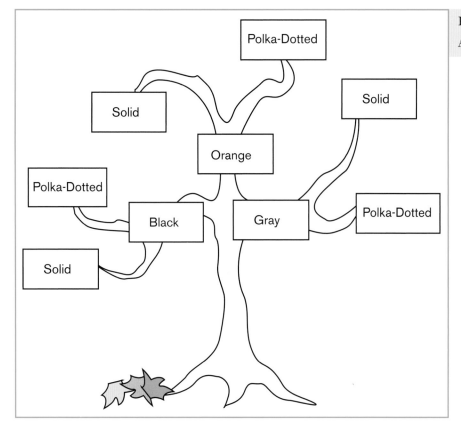

Fig. **4.**

A tree diagram

branch labeled "Orange." When it reaches the next set of branches, which are thinner, it will have to decide whether to choose the branch labeled "Solid" or the one labeled "Polka-Dotted." Hand one of the hats to a student, and have him or her follow along the branches until reaching the proper branch for the hat. It is important for the student to begin at the bottom of the tree and work up through the thick inner branches to the thinner (outer) branches. Call on different students to place the remaining hats, and ask them questions like the following to help them understand the process:

- "How do you know where to place the hat?"
- "Can one hat belong in more than one place?" (no)
- "Will two hats ever belong on the same branch?" (no) "Why or why not?" (because all the hats are different)
- "What clue could you give to a friend who does not know where to place a hat?"

Change the labels on the tree, and call on other students to place the hats. When the students can complete this task easily, select a student to help you secretly label the branches of the tree. Place the labels facing the board so that the other students cannot see them. Then place three of the hats on the thinner (outer) branches according to the hidden rules. You might, for example, place the hats as shown in figure 5.

Challenge the students to place the remaining hats according to the new, "hidden" rules. The new rules for the thicker branches are, from left to right, "orange," "gray", "black." For the thinner branches, the rules, from left to right, are "solid," "polka-dotted," "solid," "polka-dotted," "solid," "polka-dotted."

Fig. **5.**

A tree diagram with some hats. Students must infer the rules from the placement of the hats.

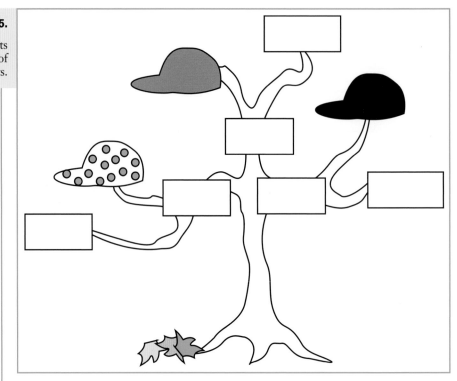

After the students demonstrate confidence in their abilities to place six hats, tell them that you would like to play the game with more hats. Have available the hats you have copied at a reduced size. Ask the students, "If I add a set of small hats that also are black, orange, or gray and solid or polka-dotted, how do you know that there will be six more? How many hats will I have all together?" (12) Show the students the set of six smaller hats that you have prepared. Draw another tree with branches identical to those for the first one, place it next to the original tree, and connect them so that you have a single tree (see fig. 6). Place the label "Large" at the bottom of the thickest left-hand branch and the label "Small" at the bottom of the thickest right-hand branch. The other labels can be placed as they were on the original tree (see fig. 6). Challenge the students to find the correct locations for the hats according to the labels. Talk about why the branches must be chosen in order, moving from thickest to thinnest. Both the thickest branches have thinner branches that have the same names; the only distinguishing attribute is the size of the hats on the tree. To increase the challenge, change the labels on the tree, and repeat the task.

Extend

Students who have been successful at playing the game with both six and twelve hats might enjoy the challenge of creating their own game. Give them the blackline master "Attribute Trees," and have them label each tree with the attributes of a different object. The students should then draw and cut out objects with the various combinations of attributes and challenge other students to place the objects on the trees.

Discussion

Teachers should continually seek ways to challenge students to stretch their problem-solving abilities. Once the students are confident

The applet Shape Sorter, on the CD-ROM, offers more practice in sorting. It allows students to sort objects of different shapes, sizes, and colors into Venn diagrams.

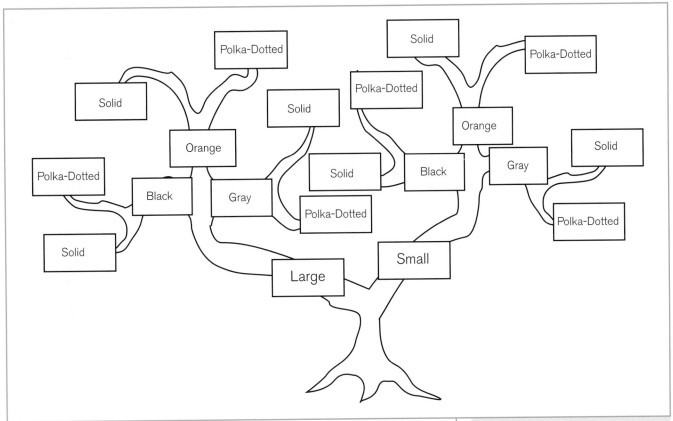

Fig. **6.**

Adding the attributes large and small creates a greater challenge for students.

about placing hats on the trees, the game can be made more challenging by turning the labels, as described in the "Explore" section. The students must then infer the rules by noticing where a few hats on the tree are placed or by counting the total number of branches to determine where there are two choices and where there are three choices.

PROBLEM SOLVING *and* REASONING

Looking Back and Looking Ahead

Navigating through Problem Solving and Reasoning in Grade 2 gives students opportunities to use a number of problem-solving strategies and reasoning methods in the content areas of number, algebra, geometry, measurement, and data. In the investigation Piggy Bank, students reason about number relationships as they use inference to decide what values might be appropriate in a particular situation and as they draw analogies between problems. They observe the usefulness of the "guess, check, and revise" strategy and are encouraged to verify their solutions. In the algebraic investigation What's the Sum? they practice deductive and analogical reasoning when they identify and use number relationships to solve problems. Students use the "guess, check, and revise" strategy again in Match Me, in which they identify three-dimensional shapes from information about the characteristics of the shapes, and they draw analogies between similar problems that involve spatial concepts. Students develop and test conjectures and use rudimentary reasoning about proportional relationships among measurements in From Small to Tall. In Hats Off, a data investigation, they reason inferentially to eliminate possible solutions and use analogies to solve different but related problems.

In grade 3, students will continue to develop their problem-solving strategies and reasoning methods as they apply what they have learned to new, grade-appropriate content. For instance, they could explore place-value relationships by manually operating a pedometer that they have made. They should have many opportunities to make and test conjectures. They might predict the effects of cutting geometric shapes or estimate the number of nonstandard units of weight that would be required to sink a boat. Students' metacognitive processes can be enhanced in a variety of activities with data, such as an investigation in which students first develop a point system for awarding certificates and then reflect on the system they have created. In an algebraic investigation, they might analyze change in order to make generalizations about number patterns. As students advance through the grades, they will refine and extend their problem-solving strategies and reasoning methods and apply them to increasingly challenging problems.

NAVIGATIONS SERIES

GRADE 2

PROBLEM SOLVING and REASONING

Appendix

Blackline Masters and Solutions

My Piggy Bank

What is the value of each of the coins?

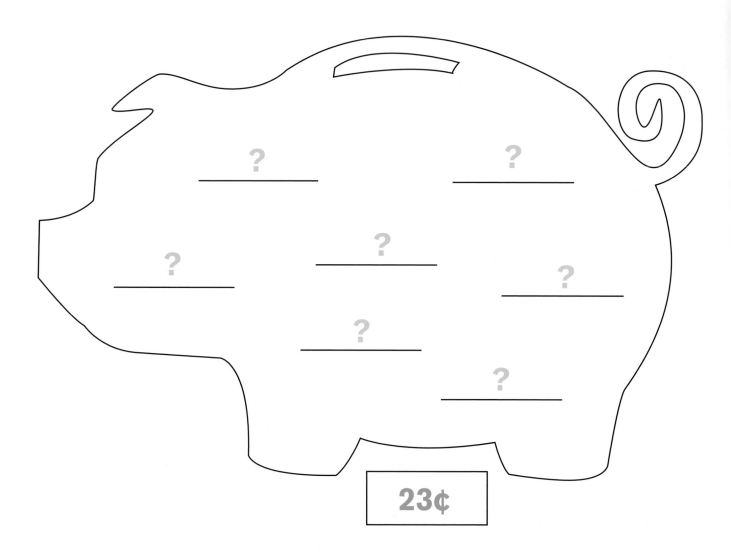

23¢

Navigating through Problem Solving and Reasoning in Grade 2

What's in the Bank?

Name _____

Write the values of the coins on the blank lines.

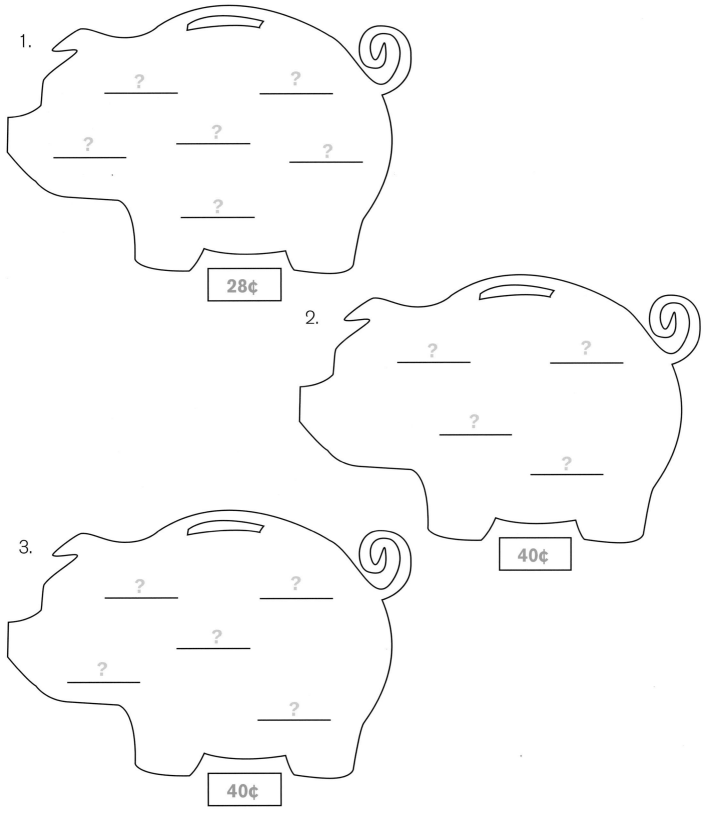

1.

? _____   ? _____

? _____   ? _____   ? _____

? _____

28¢

2.

? _____   ? _____

? _____

? _____

40¢

3.

? _____   ? _____

? _____

? _____

? _____

40¢

What's in the Bank? (continued)

Name _____

Write the values of the coins on the blank lines.

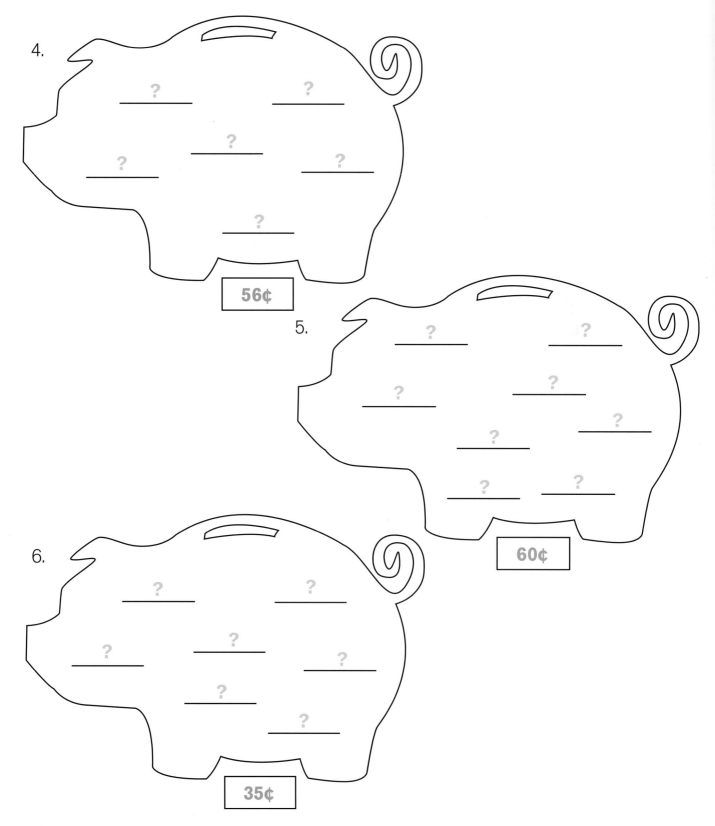

4.

? ? ? ? ? ?

56¢

5.

? ? ? ? ? ? ?

60¢

6.

? ? ? ? ? ?

35¢

Addition Grids

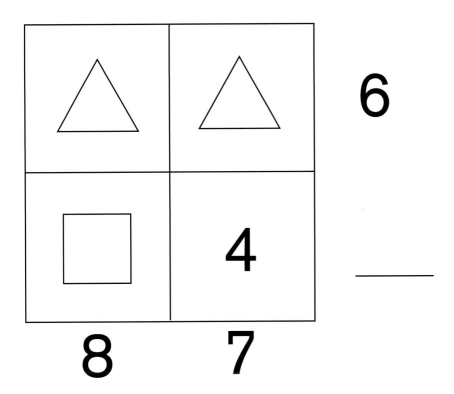

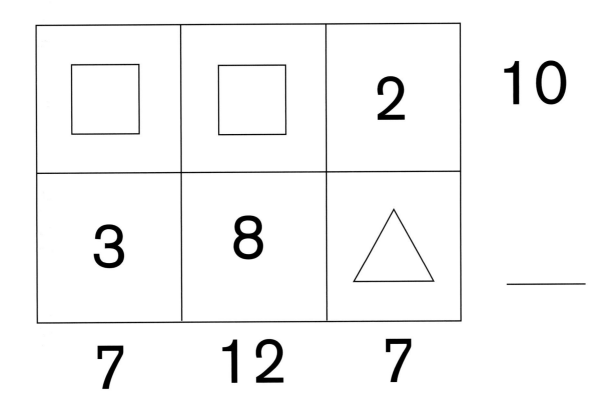

What's the Sum?

Name _____

Find the missing sums of the rows or columns. Tell which sum you found first and explain why.

1.

```
 ┌─────┬─────┐
 │  △  │  6  │  ___
 ├─────┼─────┤
 │  □  │  □  │  14
 └─────┴─────┘
   16    13
```

Row or column used first: _____

Why? _____

_____

_____

_____

2.

```
 ┌─────┬─────┐
 │  △  │  4  │  12
 ├─────┼─────┤
 │  7  │  □  │
 └─────┴─────┘  ___
   15    14
```

Row or column used first: _____

Why? _____

_____

_____

_____

3.

```
 ┌─────┬─────┐
 │  △  │  7  │  16
 ├─────┼─────┤
 │  □  │  □  │  20
 └─────┴─────┘
   ___   17
```

Row or column used first: _____

Why? _____

_____

_____

What's the Sum? (continued)

Name ______________________________

4.

□	7	18
□	△	20
22	___	

Row or column used first: ___________

Why? ______________________________

____

____

____

5.

□	2	4	13
6	△	△	___
13	10	12	

Row or column used first: ___________

Why? ______________________________

____

____

____

6.

□	4	□	14
△	△	△	12
___	8	___	

Row or column used first: ___________

Why? ______________________________

____

____

____

Shape Card 1

This square is one of the faces of a 3-D shape.

Shape Card 2

This square is one of the faces of the 3-D shape. The 3-D shape has five vertices.

Match-Me Cards

For each card, decide which three-dimensional shapes match the description. Identify as many shapes as possible. Each solid must match all the faces or conditions on the card. Build each shape that you identify.

1.

> This triangle is one of the faces of a 3-D shape.
>
>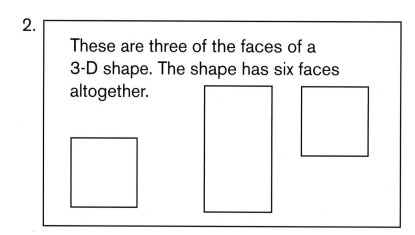

2.

> These are three of the faces of a 3-D shape. The shape has six faces altogether.

3.

> This is one of the faces of a 3-D shape. The 3-D shape has four vertices.

Match-Me Cards (continued)

Names _____

_____

4.

These are three of the faces of a 3-D shape. The 3-D shape has five faces altogether.

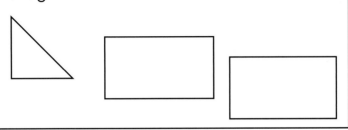

5.

These are two of the faces of a 3-D shape. The missing faces are rectangles.

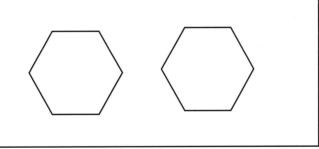

6.

This is one of the faces of a 3-D shape. The 3-D shape has twelve edges.

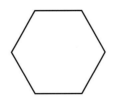

Unit Lengths

A

B

C

D

E

Navigating through Problem Solving and Reasoning in Grade 2

Body Building

ames _____

Circle the figure that your group is drawing.

Arms	Legs
3 B strips	1 B strip
4 D strips	7 C strips
9 C strips	8 D strips
15 A strips	9 A strips

Torso	Head
3 C strips	2 E strips
3 E strips	9 B strips
6 D strips	7 A strips
7 A strips	2 C strips

Hats Off

Name _____

Color these hats as your teacher asks you to do.

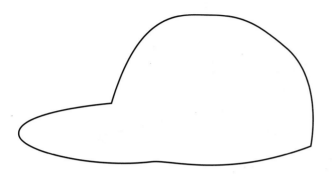

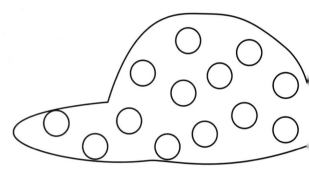

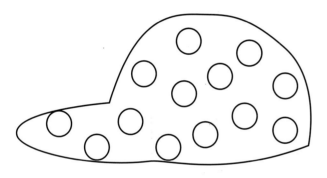

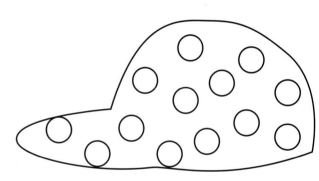

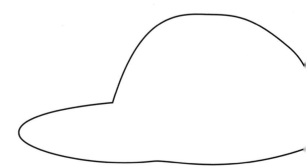

Navigating through Problem Solving and Reasoning in Grade 2

Attribute Trees

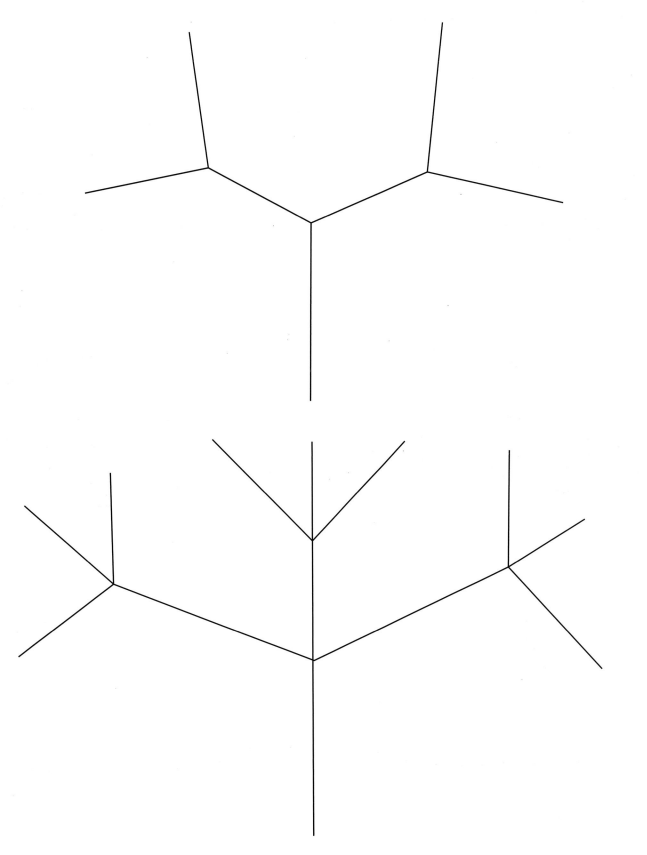

Solutions for Blackline Masters

Solutions for "What's in the Bank?"

1. 10¢, 10¢, 5¢, 1¢, 1¢, 1¢

2. 10¢, 10¢, 10¢, 10¢ or 25¢, 5¢, 5¢, 5¢

3. 10¢, 10¢, 10¢, 5¢, 5¢

4. 25¢, 10¢, 10¢, 5¢, 5¢, 1¢

5. 10¢, 10¢, 10¢, 10¢, 5¢, 5¢, 5¢, 5¢ or 25¢, 25¢, 5¢, 1¢, 1¢,1¢,1¢,1¢ or 25¢, 5¢, 5¢, 5¢, 5¢, 5¢, 5¢, 5¢

6. 25¢, 5¢, 1¢, 1¢,1¢,1¢,1¢ or 5¢, 5¢, 5¢, 5¢, 5¢, 5¢, 5¢

Solutions for "What's the Sum?"

1.

△9	6	15
7	7	14
16	13	

2.

△8	4	12
7	10	17
15	14	

3.

△9	7	16
10	10	20
19	17	

4.

11	7	18
11	△9	20
22	16	

5.

7	2	4	13
6	△8	△8	22
13	10	12	

6.

5	4	5	14
△4	△4	△4	12
9	8	9	

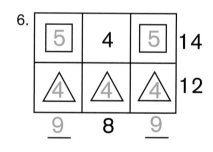

Solutions for "Match-Me Cards"

1. The possibilities include any pyramid as well as an octahedron, any triangular prism, and an icosahedron.
2. The possibilities are a right square prism and an oblique square prism.
3. The possibilities are right and oblique triangular pyramids.
4. The 3-D shape is a right triangular prism.
5. The 3-D shape is a right hexagonal prism.
6. The possibilities are right and oblique hexagonal pyramids.

Solutions for "Body Building"

	Arms	Legs	Torso	Head
by	3B	9A	7A	7A
	4D	7C	3E	2C
sketball Player	9C	8D	6D	2E

References

National Council of Teachers of Mathematics (NCTM). *Agenda for Action.* Reston, Va.: NCTM, 1980.

———. *Curriculum and Evaluation Standards for School Mathematics.* Reston, Va.: NCTM, 1989.

———. *Principles and Standards for School Mathematics.* Reston, Va.: NCTM, 2000.

Slobodkina, Esphyr. *Caps for Sale: A Tale of a Peddler, Some Monkeys, and Their Monkey Business.* New York: HarperTrophy, 1987.

Van de Walle, John A. *Elementary and Middle School Mathematics: Teaching Developmentally.* 5th ed. Boston: Allyn & Bacon, 2004.

Suggested Reading

Ameis, Jerry A. "Stories Invite Children to Solve Mathematical Problems." *Teaching Children Mathematics* 8 (January 2002): 260–64.

Atkinson, Sue. *Mathematics with Reason: The Emergent Approach to Primary Maths.* Portsmouth, N.H.: Heinemann, 1992.

Bamberger, Honi, and Patricia Hughes. *Great Glyphs around the Year.* New York: Scholastic, 2001.

Banchoff, Thomas F. "The Mathematician as a Child and Children as Mathematicians." *Teaching Children Mathematics* 6 (February 2000): 350–56.

Becker, Jerry P., and Shigeru Shimada, eds. *The Open-Ended Approach: A New Proposal for Teaching Mathematics.* Reston, Va.: National Council of Teachers of Mathematics, 1997.

Bird, Elliott. "What's in the Box? A Problem-Solving Lesson and a Discussion about Teaching." *Teaching Children Mathematics* 5 (May 1999): 504–7.

Cobb, Paul, Erna Yackel, Terry Wood, Grayson Wheatley, and Graceann Merkel. "Creating a Problem-Solving Atmosphere." *Arithmetic Teacher* 36 (September 1988): 46–47.

Dacey, Linda, and Rebeka Eston. *Show and Tell: Representing and Communicating Mathematical Ideas in K–2 Classrooms.* Sausalito, Calif.: Math Solutions, 2002.

Dacey, Linda, Carol Findell, Carole Greenes, and Rika Spungin. *Groundworks: Reasoning about Measurement, Grade 2.* Chicago, Ill.: Creative Publications, 2003.

Dacey, Linda Schulman, and Rebeka Eston. *Growing Mathematical Ideas in Kindergarten.* Sausalito, Calif.: Math Solutions, 1999.

Fielker, David. *Extending Mathematical Ability through Whole Class Teaching.* London: Hodder & Stoughton, 1997.

Findell, Carol, Linda Dacey, Carole Greenes, and Rika Spungin. *Groundworks: Reasoning about Measurement, Grade 1.* Chicago, Ill.: Creative Publications, 2003.

Findell, Carol R., Marian Small, Mary Cavanagh, Linda Dacey, Carole E. Greenes, and Linda Jensen Sheffield. *Navigating through Geometry in Prekindergarten–Grade 2.* Principles and Standards for School Mathematics Navigations Series. Reston, Va.: National Council of Teachers of Mathematics, 2001.

Frakes, Cyndi, and Kate Kline. "Teaching Young Mathematicians: The Challenges and Rewards." *Teaching Children Mathematics* 6 (February 2000): 376–81.

 Greenes, Carole. "Ready to Learn: Developing Young Children's Mathematical Powers." In *Mathematics in the Early Years*, edited by Juanita V. Copley, pp. 39–47. Reston, Va.: National Council of Teachers of Mathematics; Washington, D.C.: National Association for the Education of Young Children, 1999.

Greenes, Carole, Mary Cavanagh, Linda Dacey, Carol Findell, and Marian Small. *Navigating through Algebra in Prekindergarten–Grade 2. Principles and Standards for School Mathematics* Navigations Series. Reston, Va.: National Council of Teachers of Mathematics, 2001.

Greenes, Carole, and Carol Findell. *Groundworks: Algebraic Thinking, Grade 1.* Chicago, Ill.: Creative Publications, 1998.

——. *Groundworks: Algebraic Thinking, Grade 2.* Chicago, Ill.: Creative Publications, 1998.

Kajander, Ann E. "Creating Opportunities for Children to Think Mathematically." *Teaching Children Mathematics* 5 (April 1999): 480–86.

 Leitze, Annette Ricks. "Connecting Process Problem Solving to Children's Literature." *Teaching Children Mathematics* 7 (March 1997): 398–406.

 Myren, Christina L. "Encouraging Young Children to Solve Problems Independently." *Teaching Children Mathematics* 3 (October 1996): 72–76.

Schielack, Jane F., Dinah Chancellor, and Kimberly M. Childs. "Designing Questions to Encourage Children's Mathematical Thinking." *Teaching Children Mathematics* 6 (February 2000): 398–402.

 Sheffield, Linda Jensen. "Creating and Developing Promising Young Mathematicians." *Teaching Children Mathematics* 6 (February 2000): 416–19, 426.

Sheffield, Linda Jensen, Mary Cavanagh, Linda Dacey, Carol R. Findell, Carole E. Greenes, and Marian Small. *Navigating through Data Analysis and Probability in Prekindergarten—Grade 2. Principles and Standards for School Mathematics* Navigations Series. Reston, Va.: National Council of Teachers of Mathematics, 2002.

 Sophian, Catherine. "Children's Ways of Knowing: Lessons from Cognitive Development Research." In *Mathematics in the Early Years*, edited by Juanita V. Copley, pp. 11–20. Reston, Va.: National Council of Teachers of Mathematics; Washington, D.C.: National Association for the Education of Young Children, 1999.

 Whitenack, Joy, and Erna Yackel. "Making Mathematical Arguments in the Primary Grades: The Importance of Explaining and Justifying Ideas." *Teaching Children Mathematics* 8 (May 2002): 524–27.

Young, Cindy, and Wendy Maulding. "Mathematics and Mother Goose." *Teaching Children Mathematics* 1 (September 1994): 36–38.